A Mosquito in the Cabin

Poems chosen by
Richard Brown and Kate Ruttle

Illustrated by Amanda Hall
and Susan Hellard

CAMBRIDGE
UNIVERSITY PRESS

Cambridge Reading

General Editors
Richard Brown and Kate Ruttle

Consultant Editor
Jean Glasberg

Published by the Press Syndicate of the University of Cambridge
The Pitt Building, Trumpington Street, Cambridge CB2 1RP
40 West 20th Street, New York, NY10011-4211, USA
10 Stamford Road, Oakleigh, Melbourne 3166, Australia

First published 1996

A Mosquito in the Cabin
This selection © Richard Brown and Kate Ruttle 1996
Illustrations © Amanda Hall and Susan Hellard 1996

Printed in Great Britain at the University Press, Cambridge

A catalogue record for this book is available from the British Library

ISBN 0 521 49989 5 paperback

Acknowledgements

We are grateful to the following for permission to reproduce poems:
'The Fly' by Tony Bradman from *Smile, Please!* by Tony Bradman. © Tony Bradman
   1987. First published in Viking Children's Books. Reprinted by permission of Penguin
   Books Ltd.
'The Silverfish' © Richard Brown 1996.
'Afternoon' and 'Earth-Worm' by Leonard Clark. Reproduced by permission of Robert
   Clark, The Literary Executor of Leonard Clark.
'Bee' and 'Beetle' © John Cotton 1996.
'Giant', 'Butterfly' and 'Spider' by June Crebbin from *The Dinosaur's Dinner* by June
   Crebbin. © June Crebbin 1992. First published in Viking Children's Books 1992.
   Reprinted by permission of Penguin Books Ltd.
'Giant Moth' by June Crebbin from *The Jungle Sale* by June Crebbin, published by Viking
   Kestrel 1988. © June Crebbin 1988.
'The Dragonfly' by Eleanor Farjeon from *Silver Sand and Snow*, published by Michael
   Joseph.
'Fireflies' by J. Patrick Lewis. First published in *A Cup of Starshine*, Walker Books 1991.
'Insect' © Tony Mitton 1996.
'The Ground' by Tatsuji Miyoshi from *An Anthology of Modern Japanese Poetry*
   translated and edited by I. Kono and R. Fukuda 1957.
'Don't Cry Caterpillar' © Grace Nichols 1991. Reproduced with permission of Curtis
   Brown Group Ltd, London, on behalf of Grace Nichols.
'Mosquito in the Cabin' by Myra Stilborn from *Round Slice of Moon* © 1980 Scholastic
   TAB Publications Ltd. Reprinted by permission of the author.
'Crickets' by Valerie Worth from *Small Poems*. Poems © 1972 by Valerie Worth.
   Reprinted by permission of Farrar, Straus & Giroux Inc.

Every effort has been made to reach copyright holders; the publishers would like to hear
from anyone whose rights they have unknowingly infringed.

Contents

Giant

There's a giant in our classroom,
He comes from far away,
We've made him warm and comfortable,
We're hoping that he'll stay.

He wears a suit of armour
To shield him from attack,
It's hard to tell which part of him
Is front and which is back.

He keeps himself inside himself
Until he moves about,
When eyes and head and everything
Gently ripple out.

His giant foot begins to spread,
His giant eyes explore,
And when he's eaten all there is
He looks around for more.

He waves his giant feelers,
He leaves a giant trail,
I never tire of watching
Our Giant African Snail!

June Crebbin

The Caterpillar

Brown and furry
Caterpillar in a hurry;
Take your walk
To the shady leaf or stalk.

May no toad spy you,
May the little birds pass by you;
Spin and die,
To live again a butterfly.

Christina Rossetti

Don't Cry, Caterpillar

Don't cry, Caterpillar
Caterpillar, don't cry
You'll be a butterfly – by and by.

Caterpillar, please
Don't worry 'bout a thing

"But," said Caterpillar,
"Will I still know myself – in wings?"

Grace Nichols

Butterfly

This morning I found a butterfly
Against my bedroom wall.

I wanted to hold it,
To remember its colours.

But instead I guided its whirring shape
Towards the open window.

I watched it drift into the warm air,
Swaying and looping across the summer garden.

In my book I found:
'Tortoiseshell, reddish-orange with yellow
patches.'

But I remember its leaving,
And the pattern of its moving.

June Crebbin

The Fly

Zzzzzzzzzzzzzz . . .

There's a fly inside my bedroom,
It's driving me insane;
It's buzzing round my wardrobe,
It's on the window pane . . .

It's flying round the lampshade,
It's coming very close.
It's landed on my pillow . . .
It's walking on my nose!

It's looking in my eyeball,
Phew! It's flying off again!
It's walking on the ceiling,
It's driving me insane!

It's buzzing and it's buzzing,
It's coming near again,
I'll never, ever, get to sleep.
That fly is such a pain!

It's buzzing round the bedpost,
It's walking on the floor . . .
It's flying round my toys and, yes!
It's buzzing out the door.

The fly's buzzed off and left me,
So now I'll close my eyes . . .
But wait . . . do I hear buzzing?
It's back, surprise, surprise!

Zzzzzzzzzzzzzzz . . .

Tony Bradman

The Visitor

one night
i woke up
when the
rest were
asleep
and felt
something
crawly
that started
to creep
up my arm
'neath the
covers
i brushed
it away
but it
didn't go
it wanted
to stay
it creepy
crawled
slowly
with long
hair
steps

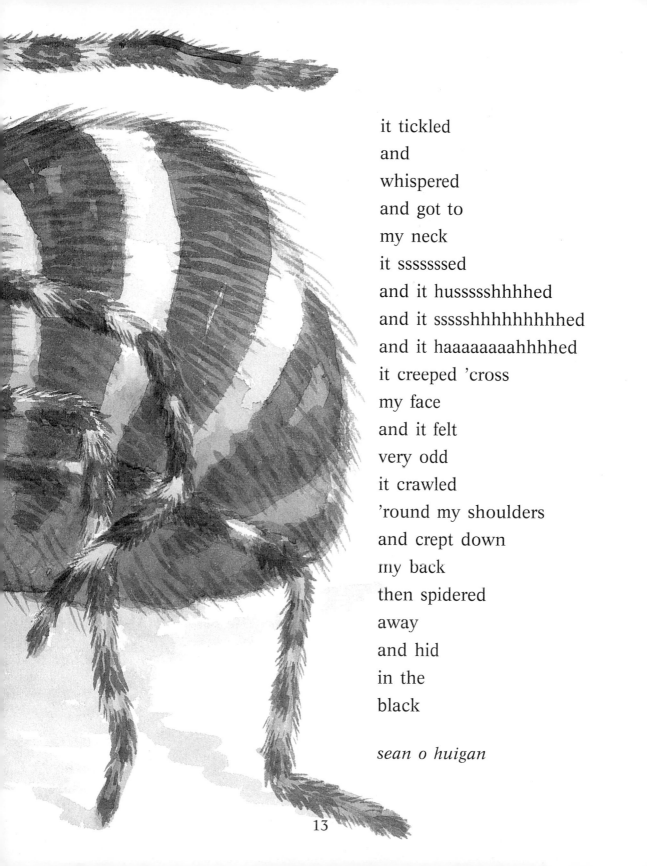

it tickled
and
whispered
and got to
my neck
it ssssssed
and it hussssshhhhed
and it sssssshhhhhhhhhed
and it haaaaaaaahhhhed
it creeped 'cross
my face
and it felt
very odd
it crawled
'round my shoulders
and crept down
my back
then spidered
away
and hid
in the
black

sean o huigan

Spider

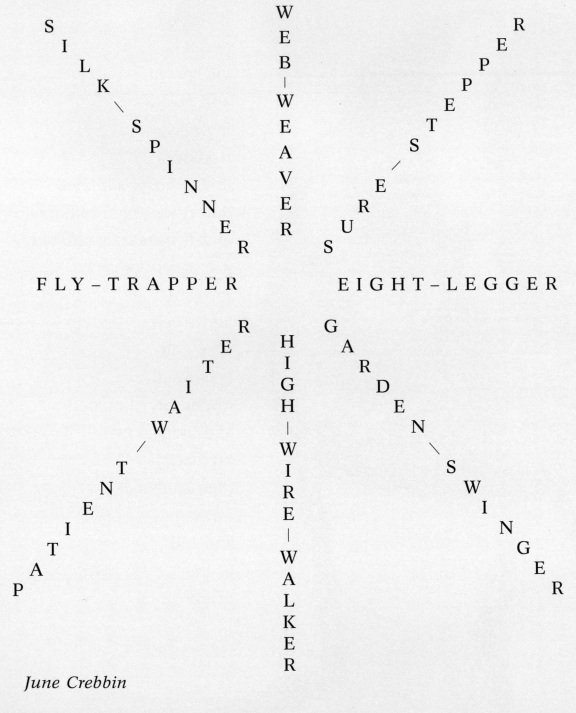

SILK SPINNER

WEB-WEAVER

SURE-STEPPER

FLY–TRAPPER

EIGHT–LEGGER

PATIENT WAITER

HIGH-WIRE-WALKER

GARDEN SWINGER

June Crebbin

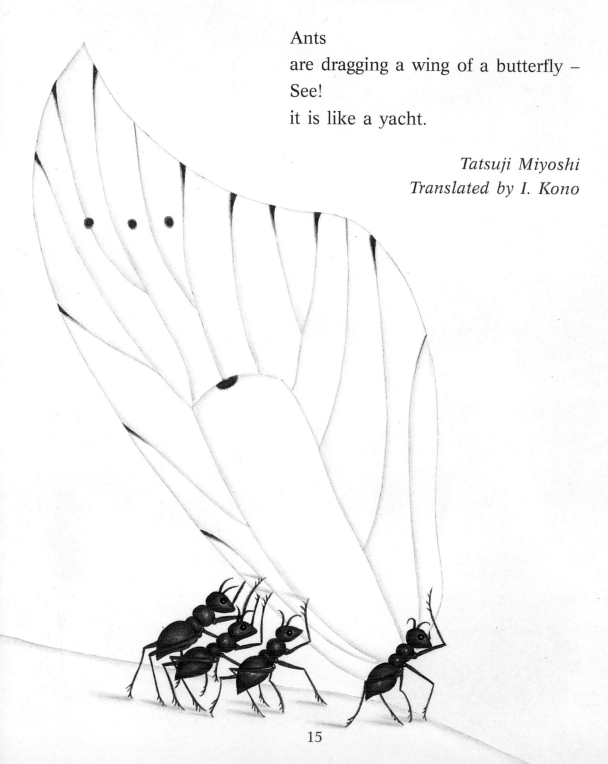

The Ground

Ants
are dragging a wing of a butterfly –
See!
it is like a yacht.

Tatsuji Miyoshi
Translated by I. Kono

Bee

Busy buzzer
Busy bee,
Making honey
For our tea,
Cheerful in your
Striped jersey.

John Cotton

Afternoon

Four o'clock. The afternoon is asleep,
A bee hums in the long grasses,
A hill is white with drowsy sheep;
So slowly each hour passes
With shadows falling
On soundless butterfly
Floating into the dreaming sky.

Leonard Clark

Insect

Inspect
an insect
and you'll see
how pretty
it can be.
Listen,
and hear
the tiny song
it sings.
And see the rainbows
glisten
on its wings.

Tony Mitton

18

The Silverfish

When we turned the mattress
on my bed this morning
a little torpedo of a
                silverfish
                    zig-zagged
                        across the
                            mattress
                                in a frenzy
                            at being caught
                        there.
            I shrieked,
            and tried to hit it
        but it zig-zagged so fast
I missed,
        puffing up
            clouds of dust
                that made my mum
                    complain.
                        The silverfish
                    found a little hole
                in the mattress
        and disappeared.
            It's inside there
                somewhere,
                    disturbing my dreams.

Richard Brown

Giant Moth

One windy day,
when I was taking a message
across to the Infant School
with my friend,

I saw
a giant moth
land
on the school field.

It was so big
I could see clearly
its yellow and brown markings.

As it rested
I saw
each wing lift
and tremble
before it rose in the air again.

My friend said
it was only a big leaf,

But I said,
I think I know a Giant Moth
when I see one.

June Crebbin

Earth-Worm

Do
you
squirm
when
you
see
an earth-worm?
I never
do squirm
because I think
a big fat worm
is really rather clever
the way it can shrink
and go
so small
without
a sound
into the ground.
And then
what about
all
that
work it does
and no oxygen
or miner's hat?
Marvellous
you have to admit,
even if you don't like fat
pink worms a bit,

how with that
thin
slippery skin
it makes its way
day after day
through the soil,
such honest toil.
And don't forget
the dirt
it eats, I bet
you wouldn't like to come out
at night to squirt
it all over the place
with no eyes in your face:
I doubt
too if you know
an earth-worm is deaf, but
it can hear YOU go
to and fro
even if you cut
it in half.
Do not laugh
or squirm
again
when
you
suddenly
see
a worm.

Leonard Clark

Crickets

Crickets
Talk
In the tall
Grass
All
Late summer
Long.
When
Summer
Is gone,
The dry
Grass
Whispers
Alone.

Valerie Worth

Beetle

Glossy black beetle,
Carefully walking
In your forest of grass.
A nest of leaves,
A crack in the wall,
You'rc safe home at last!

John Cotton

A Mosquito in the Cabin

Although you bash her,
    swat her, smash her,
and go to bed victorious,
    happy and glorious
      she will come winging
      zooming and zinging,
      wickedly singing
over your bed.

You slap the air
    but she's in your hair
    cackling with laughter.
You smack your head,
    but she isn't dead –
    she's on the rafter.
She's out for your blood –
    yours, my friend,
and she will get it, in the end.
She brings it first to boiling point,
    then lets it steam.
With fee, fi, fo and contented fum
    she sips it
    while you dream.

Myra Stilborn

The Dragonfly

When the heat of the summer
Made drowsy the land,
A dragonfly came
And sat on my hand,
With its blue jointed body,
And wings like spun glass,
It lit on my fingers
As though they were grass.

Eleanor Farjeon

Fireflies

An August night –
The wind not quite
A wind, the sky
Not just a sky –
And everywhere
The speckled air
Of summer stars
Alive in jars.

J. Patrick Lewis

Ladybird! Ladybird!

Ladybird! Ladybird! Fly away home,
Night is approaching, and sunset is come:
The herons are flown to their trees by the Hall;
Felt, but unseen, the damp dewdrops fall.
This is the close of a still summer day;
Ladybird! Ladybird! Haste! Fly away!

Emily Brontë

Hurt No Living Thing

Hurt no living thing,
Ladybird, nor butterfly,
Nor moth with dusty wing,
Nor cricket chirping cheerily,
Nor grasshopper so light of leap,
Nor dancing gnat,
Nor beetle fat,
Nor harmless worms that creep.

Christina Rossetti

Index of first lines